The Missing Rabbit

By Carmel Reilly

I love to stay with
my friend April.

Her family has a big yard
to play in.

And lots of animals!

April's family has two dogs,
one rabbit and some fish.

And they have a parrot
named Tulip.

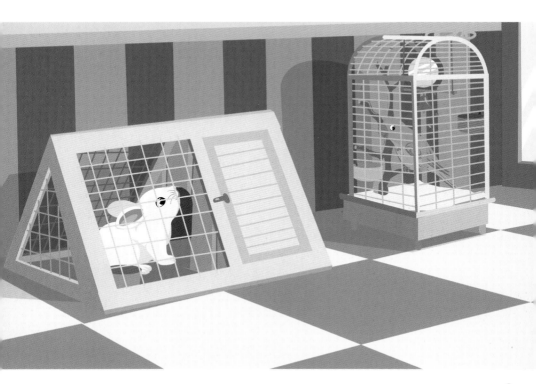

I stayed at April's house in the school holidays.

One day, I could hear April yelling.

She was in the sun room.

"What is it?" I said.

"I did not shut the pen door!"
said April.
"My rabbit Colin is missing!"

"Pen door!" yelled Tulip
the parrot.

"Shoosh, Tulip!" said April.

"Shoosh! Shoosh!"
Tulip yelled back.

"Help me look for the rabbit,"
April said.

We looked in the yard,
but we did not find him.

Tulip was still yelling out.

"Tulip is an odd bird!" I said.

"There is no exit out of here,"
April said.

"That sneaky rabbit can not
have got far."

We went back into
the sun room.

Tulip was still yelling.
"Pen door, pen door!" he said.

"Wait!" I said.
"Do you think ...?"

I went to Colin's pen
and shut the pen door.

There was Colin the rabbit.

"Colin!" April said.

"Tulip was right!" I said.

"I should not have yelled
at you, Tulip," said April.
"You can have some lentils
as a treat!"

CHECKING FOR MEANING

1. What pets does April's family have? *(Literal)*

2. How did Colin get out of the pen? *(Literal)*

3. Why was Tulip yelling, "Pen door! Pen door!"? *(Inferential)*

EXTENDING VOCABULARY

family	What is a *family*? Who makes up your family? Are all families the same?
parrot	What is a *parrot*? What does a parrot look like? What are other types of birds you know? E.g. sparrow, magpie, kookaburra, budgerigar.
exit	What is an *exit*? What do you do at an exit? What is the opposite of an exit?

MOVING BEYOND THE TEXT

1. Talk about different birds that can mimic human speech. What words do they often say? Why?

2. Make a list of animals and where they live, e.g. dog – kennel; horse – stable; bear – den.

3. Discuss why some pets need to be kept in a pen or cage. What might have happened to Colin if he got out of the cage?

4. Do you have pets? What are suitable treats to give them? How can you use treats to train a pet?

THE SCHWA

| a | e | i | o | u |

PRACTICE WORDS

a

the

April

rabbit

family

parrot

holidays

Tulip

lentils

Colin

exit

animals

April's